COUNTRY KNOWLEDGE PLAN PROCESS MANUAL

DEVELOPING A DYNAMIC COUNTRY KNOWLEDGE PLAN FOR ADB DEVELOPING MEMBER COUNTRIES

JUNE 2022

ASIAN DEVELOPMENT BANK

Contents

Tables and Figures

Acknowledgments

This Country Knowledge Plan Process Manual is the result of the collaborative efforts of the Strategy, Policy and Partnerships Department (SPD) and the Knowledge Advisory Services Center at the Sustainable Development and Climate Change Department (SDCC-KC) of the Asian Development Bank.

Authors:

Vivek Raman

Mary Jane Carangal-San Jose

Pronita Agrawal

Ashwath Dasarathy

Production managers:

Susann Roth

Vivek Raman

The following provided valuable inputs in the preparation of the manual:

David Daniel Oldfield

Lindsay Marie Renaud

Josephine J. Aquino

Manuscript editors:

Jane Parry and Levi Lusterio

Layout design:

Insomniac Design, Inc.

Abbreviations

ADB	Asian Development Bank
ADBI	Asian Development Bank Institute
CKP	country knowledge plan
CPM	country programming mission
CPS	country partnership strategy
DMC	developing member country
ICPM	indicative country pipeline and monitoring report
KPS	knowledge products and services
PSOD	Private Sector Operations Department
RETA	regional technical assistance
SDCC-KC	Sustainable Development and Climate Change Department, Knowledge Advisory Services Center
TA	technical assistance

I. Overview

A. Why Prepare a Country Knowledge Plan?

1. The Asian Development Bank's (ADB) Strategy 2030 aims to strengthen its country-focused approach using the country partnership strategy (CPS) as the main platform to provide lending and knowledge support to its developing member countries (DMCs).[1]

2. The CPS is a directional document that sets out the strategic framework for ADB's operational support to its DMCs. Introduced in 2015, the country knowledge plan (CKP) is an appendix to the CPS that outlines the country's knowledge needs over the CPS period. However, the CKP has been traditionally viewed as a separate exercise to country programming.

3. The "dynamic" CKP process will enable country teams to address the following issues:

    (i) The previous CKP was focused on individual knowledge products and services (KPS), and was often unclear how the CKP met the needs of the DMC. The new CKP process emphasizes a programmatic approach to deliver knowledge to ensure that the technical assistance (TA) projects used to produce these KPS are not implemented in siloes. The dynamic CKP focuses on achieving knowledge outcomes that are linked to the CPS strategic objectives that address development challenges in DMCs and address Paris Agreement alignment upstream.

    (ii) The previous CKP emphasized counting the number of KPS, instead of focusing on knowledge solutions. The dynamic CKP emphasizes quality rather than quantity to demonstrate how ADB's knowledge is helping DMCs solve challenges along the following key knowledge result categories: (a) increasing awareness and evidence-based information, (b) improving program or project delivery, and (c) enhancing capacities and skills in the DMCs.

    (iii) In the previous CKP, the link between upstream knowledge and future lending is not clear. The new dynamic CKP ensures ADB's knowledge TA portfolio is balanced between government demand and the bank's proposed knowledge support. This requires improved collaboration within ADB and with the respective DMC government.

4. The conduct of more frequent or regular consultations on knowledge with the clients and prioritizing what ADB can offer to meet their knowledge needs make the country knowledge programming process dynamic. The annual update through the indicative country pipeline and monitoring (ICPM) report ensures that the CKP is dynamic to meet any emerging and just-in-time knowledge needs from the DMCs within the CPS period.

5. This manual outlines the steps to prepare a dynamic CKP. It can also be applied by country teams that are in the midterm phase of their CPS.

---

[1] Asian Development Bank (ADB). 2018. Strategy 2030, Achieving a Prosperous, Inclusive, Resilient, and Sustainable Asia and the Pacific. Manila.

B. Responsibility for Preparing a Country Knowledge Plan

6. The CKP is developed by a team with the following roles and responsibilities:

   (i) **Regional department.** Oversees the CPS process, including the preparation of the CKP and the ICPM report.

   (ii) **Country director.** Establishes the team to prepare the CPS, CKP, and ICPM—oversees the pre-CPS work, identifies the strategic objectives of the CPS and outcomes of the CKP, and validates and prioritizes ADB's knowledge to meet the DMC's needs.

   (iii) **CPS/CKP team (or country team).** Leads the preparation of the CKP. The team identifies the DMC's knowledge needs during the country programming mission through knowledge consultations. The team collates and analyzes ADB's existing and planned knowledge support to the DMC and validates it with sector divisions, knowledge departments (Economic Research and Regional Cooperation Department (ERCD) and the Sustainable Development and Climate Change Department), the Private Sector Operations Department (PSOD), other non-operations departments who deliver knowledge support to DMCs, and the ADB Institute (ADBI).[2] The team will engage relevant departments in preparing assessments, identifying country challenges, and designing the CKP.

   (iv) **Knowledge management focal points in regional departments.** Support coordination of the dynamic CKP process for their respective resident missions.

   (v) **Sustainable Development and Climate Change Department, Knowledge Advisory Services Center (SDCC-KC).** Advises and supports the CKP teams in preparing their CKP. SDCC-KC designed several tools to assist in the analysis of knowledge support to a DMC, mapping of knowledge partnerships, and matching of knowledge supply from ADB with the knowledge needs of the government.[3]

   (vi) **Sector divisions, knowledge departments, sector and thematic groups, and other non-operations departments, including PSOD and ADBI, providing knowledge to DMCs.** Validate ADB's planned knowledge support, participate in government consultations, and help prioritize knowledge solutions in consultation with the CKP team and the DMC governments.

---

[2] Footnote 1, para. 57: "In the new CKP outline, the section on promoting knowledge as One ADB will include discussion of the measures to ensure greater collaboration across ADB and ADBI, when applicable."
[3] SDCC-KC is discussing with the Information Technology Department the use of Microsoft Power BI to facilitate the analysis of ADB's knowledge support.

II. Steps in Formulating a Dynamic Country Knowledge Plan

7. There are four steps in developing a dynamic CKP: analyze, consult, prioritize, and draft. As shown in Figure 1, these four steps need not be executed in chronological order, as these steps can be undertaken simultaneously or in conjunction with other ongoing processes.

Figure 1: Key Steps For Developing A Dynamic Country Knowledge Plan

Four Key Steps of the CKP

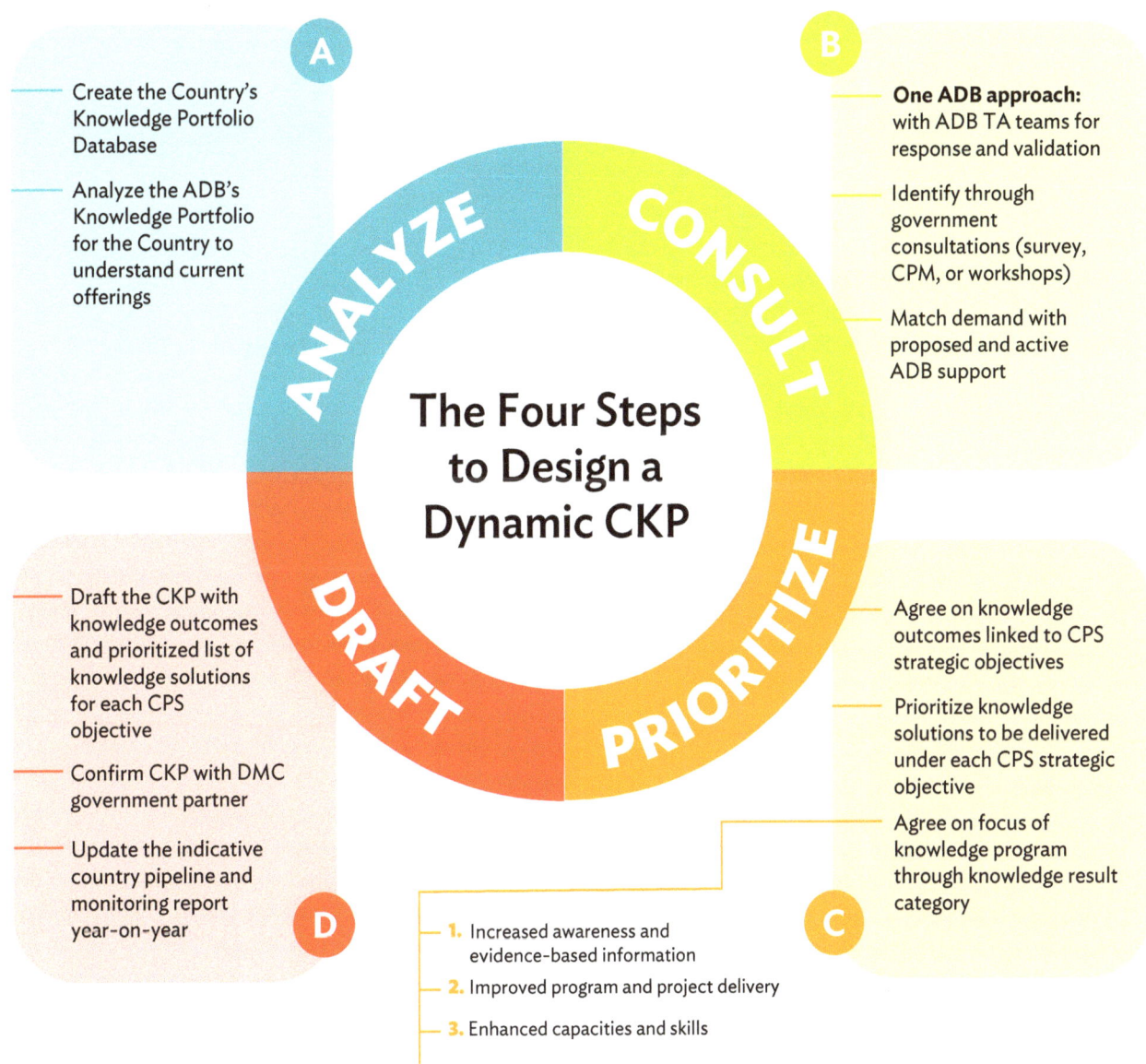

The Four Steps to Design a Dynamic CKP

A — ANALYZE
- Create the Country's Knowledge Portfolio Database
- Analyze the ADB's Knowledge Portfolio for the Country to understand current offerings

B — CONSULT
- **One ADB approach:** with ADB TA teams for response and validation
- Identify through government consultations (survey, CPM, or workshops)
- Match demand with proposed and active ADB support

C — PRIORITIZE
- Agree on knowledge outcomes linked to CPS strategic objectives
- Prioritize knowledge solutions to be delivered under each CPS strategic objective
- Agree on focus of knowledge program through knowledge result category

1. Increased awareness and evidence-based information
2. Improved program and project delivery
3. Enhanced capacities and skills

D — DRAFT
- Draft the CKP with knowledge outcomes and prioritized list of knowledge solutions for each CPS objective
- Confirm CKP with DMC government partner
- Update the indicative country pipeline and monitoring report year-on-year

ADB = Asian Development Bank, CKP = country knowledge plan, CPM = country programming mission, CPS = country partnership strategy, DMC = developing member country, TA = technical assistance.

Source: Knowledge Advisory Services Center, Sustainable Development and Climate Change Department, Asian Development Bank.

A. Analyze

1. Creating the Country's Knowledge Portfolio Database

8. Create a knowledge portfolio of the country. The CKP team, with support from SDCC-KC, can create a preliminary list of active and proposed TA projects from the ADB website (https://www.adb.org/projects). The team can refine the search by "country" and "status of the project" (i.e., active and proposed). It is useful to decide the time period to collate the TA projects to be included in the analysis. Table 1 shows the list of data points available on the ADB website that is useful for conducting analysis (CKP teams may use this Microsoft Excel template for collecting data).

TABLE 1: Data to Be Collected on Technical Assistance

Data to Be Collected
Technical Assistance (TA) number and name
Type of TA: Knowledge and Support Technical Assistance (KSTA), Transactions Technical Assistance (TRTA)
Geographic scope: Country-Specific Technical Assistance and Regional Technical Assistance (RETA)
Date of approval
Developing member countries covered, in case of RETA
Objective of the TA
Amount based on original TA report ($ million)
Amount for the specific country as per original TA report ($ million)
Fund source: Asian Development Bank (ADB) (amount and source of fund)   Fund source: Cofinancing (amount and source of fund)   Fund source: Counterpart (amount and source of fund)
Associated sector(s). If more than one, map the primary and secondary sectors.
Department in-charge
Operational priority of ADB
Link to TA report

Source: Knowledge Advisory Services Center, Sustainable Development and Climate Change Department, Asian Development Bank.

9. **Validate the knowledge portfolio.** The CKP team validates the list of TA projects generated with relevant departments to

    (i) add any missing TA projects;

    (ii) make corrections in the TA project included (amount allocated as TA funds for the project or country, including any additional financing after the published TA report);

    (iii) confirm the amount of funds allocated for the country for regional TA (RETA) projects, otherwise the default option would be to divide the total RETA amount by the number of DMCs covered by the RETA; and

    (iv) decide which RETA projects should be included in the portfolio based on

        (a) the number of DMCs included in the RETA, and/or

        (b) the approximate average value per DMC from the RETA (e.g., CKP team may include only RETA where the country received at least $100,000).

10. **Consolidate the knowledge portfolio for analysis.** The CKP team incorporates all inputs provided by departments to create the final knowledge TA portfolio for analysis.

2. Analysis of ADB's Knowledge Portfolio for the Country

11. **Analyze existing and proposed TA portfolio.** Based on the validated TA portfolio (as discussed in paras. 7-9), the CKP team (with support from SDCC-KC, if required) analyzes ADB's ongoing and proposed TA for the country. The TA portfolio analysis provides insights into ADB's current and future knowledge support, such as linkage with ADB Strategy 2030, CPS development objectives and sectoral and/or thematic focus, among others. The team can conduct the analysis separately for active and proposed TA projects using data in Appendix 1.[4]

12. **Partnership mapping.** The CKP team, with support from SDCC-KC, also needs to check the Knowledge Partnership Toolbox for any knowledge partnership that includes the DMC among its beneficiaries. The steps to follow are

    (i) go to the Knowledge Partnership Toolbox (https://partnerships.adb.org/);

    (ii) click on the "countries" tab;

    (iii) under "Partnerships Country Focus," click on the relevant DMC; and

    (iv) export the search results to Microsoft Excel.

13. The CKP team assesses the existing partnerships, whether these are country-specific or regional, and maps how these complement the knowledge provided under ADB's TA projects to fill in any knowledge gaps. This can help decide how to leverage existing partnerships for ADB's planned country operations and if new partnerships are required in any sector or thematic area to meet the CPS strategic objectives. Figure 2 shows a sample map.

---

[4] See sample portfolio analysis conducted for Sri Lanka here.

Figure 2: Sample Partnership Listing for Pacific Island Countries, 2020

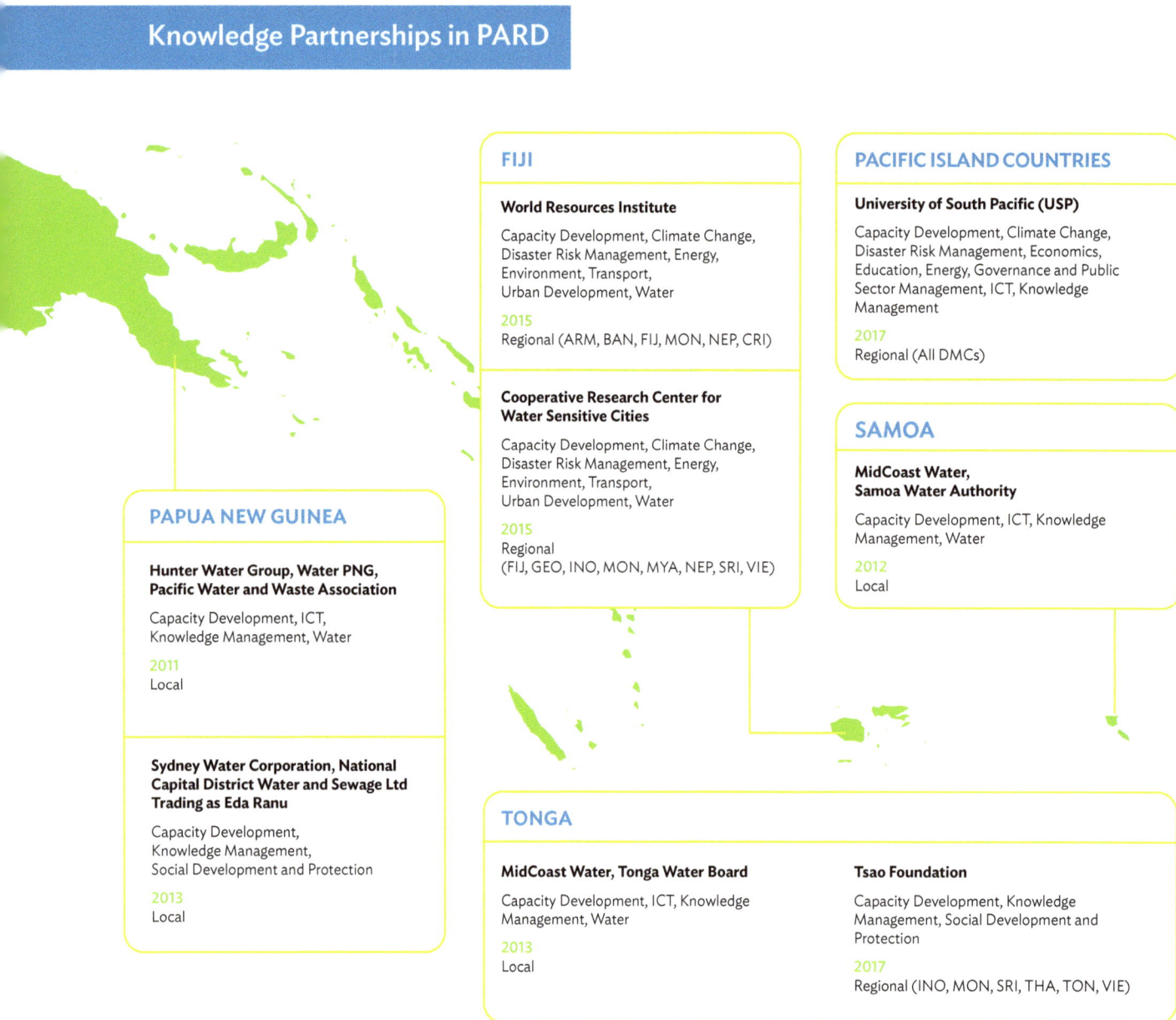

Knowledge Partnerships in PARD

FIJI

World Resources Institute

Capacity Development, Climate Change, Disaster Risk Management, Energy, Environment, Transport, Urban Development, Water

2015
Regional (ARM, BAN, FIJ, MON, NEP, CRI)

Cooperative Research Center for Water Sensitive Cities

Capacity Development, Climate Change, Disaster Risk Management, Energy, Environment, Transport, Urban Development, Water

2015
Regional
(FIJ, GEO, INO, MON, MYA, NEP, SRI, VIE)

PACIFIC ISLAND COUNTRIES

University of South Pacific (USP)

Capacity Development, Climate Change, Disaster Risk Management, Economics, Education, Energy, Governance and Public Sector Management, ICT, Knowledge Management

2017
Regional (All DMCs)

SAMOA

MidCoast Water, Samoa Water Authority

Capacity Development, ICT, Knowledge Management, Water

2012
Local

PAPUA NEW GUINEA

Hunter Water Group, Water PNG, Pacific Water and Waste Association

Capacity Development, ICT, Knowledge Management, Water

2011
Local

Sydney Water Corporation, National Capital District Water and Sewage Ltd Trading as Eda Ranu

Capacity Development, Knowledge Management, Social Development and Protection

2013
Local

TONGA

MidCoast Water, Tonga Water Board

Capacity Development, ICT, Knowledge Management, Water

2013
Local

Tsao Foundation

Capacity Development, Knowledge Management, Social Development and Protection

2017
Regional (INO, MON, SRI, THA, TON, VIE)

ARM = Armenia, BAN = Bangladesh, CRI = Costa Rica, FIJ = Fiji, GEO = Georgia, ICT = information and communication technology, INO = Indonesia, MON = Mongolia, MYA = Myanmar, NEP = Nepal, PARD = Pacific Department, PNG = Papua New Guinea, SRI = Sri Lanka, THA = Thailand, TON = Tonga, VIE = Viet Nam.

Source: Knowledge Advisory Services Center, Sustainable Development and Climate Change Department, Asian Development Bank.

B. Consult

1. Consult with ADB Technical Assistance Teams for Response and Validation

14. **ADB consultations.** The CKP team validates the analysis of the knowledge (TA) portfolio by consulting with management, relevant sector divisions, knowledge departments, sector groups, thematic groups, other non-operations departments, including PSOD and ADBI. The CKP team can decide how best to organize the consultations, ensuring a "One ADB" approach. (Appendix 3 provides a sample agenda for consultation and an e-mail to invite participants). This consultation is to validate the analysis conducted in the preceding section (paras.10–12) and seek inputs on the knowledge support, knowledge gaps (if any), and how knowledge solutions can be tailored to meet the country's knowledge needs.

2. Identify Country's Knowledge Needs through Government Consultations or Survey

15. The CKP team needs to identify the government's **development priorities and associated knowledge needs** through discussions during the country programming mission (CPM), or by organizing separate knowledge consultations based on the country context, size of the knowledge portfolio, and need. It is useful to structure these knowledge consultations around the CPS strategic objectives, and ideally to be done simultaneously with the CPM. For consultations, the team shall

    (i) select representatives from government agencies that have been involved with ADB's ongoing or planned projects;

    (ii) draft an agenda by CPS strategic objectives and/or subobjectives (Appendix 4 includes a suggested agenda and e-mail to invite government participants);

    (iii) prepare a presentation to (a) share ADB's knowledge support across TA projects, CPS strategic objectives, sectors, departments, and knowledge result categories; and (b) gather feedback and agree on a way forward (see Sample Presentation); and

    (iv) capture inputs on further knowledge needs from DMC government representatives (in case it is not captured in the CPM or through a survey discussed below).

16. Another option to gather demand from the government is through a survey. The CKP team can run the survey for up to 3 weeks.[5] The team can customize the survey (see Appendix 5 for sample survey questionnaire) to include

    (i) priority knowledge needs of the DMC's department or agency in line with national development objectives,

    (ii) corresponding knowledge solutions that could meet their knowledge needs,

    (iii) knowledge partnerships that will support the DMC in delivering knowledge solutions,

    (iv) ongoing and/or similar activities underway in the department or agency to meet the proposed knowledge outcome, and

    (v) an indicative list of areas of knowledge support provided by other partners to the agency or department.

---

[5] SDCC-KC can help design the survey and analyze the results.

3. Match Demand with Proposed and Active ADB Support

17. The country team now clusters ADB's knowledge support in response to the DMC knowledge needs (collected from government departments and agencies as discussed in para. 13) according to each CPS strategic objective. Appendix 6A provides a sample based on CPS strategic objectives. Figure 3 shows a sample of matching knowledge supply with demand from Viet Nam. The data indicates the need to meet greater demand from the DMC for knowledge to help improve program/project delivery.

FIGURE 3: Sample of Matching Supply and Demand for Knowledge

Mapping: ADB's Supply vs. Government's Demand (Viet Nam)

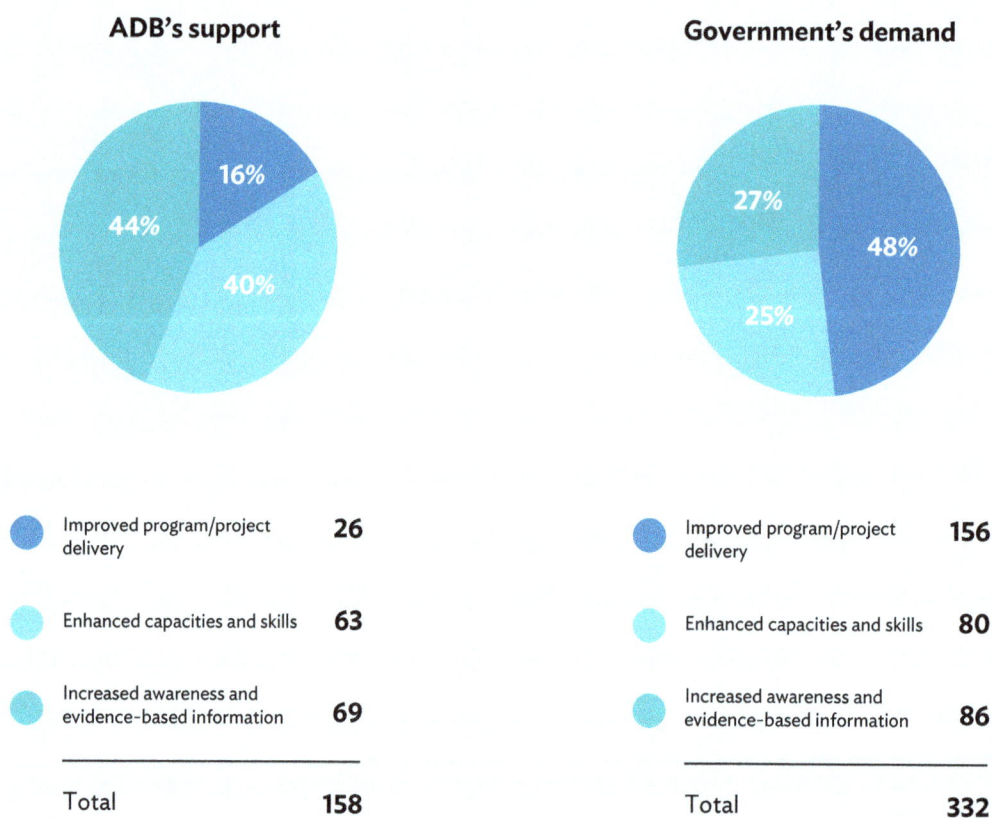

ADB's support

● Improved program/project delivery	**26**	
● Enhanced capacities and skills	**63**	
● Increased awareness and evidence-based information	**69**	
Total	**158**	

Government's demand

● Improved program/project delivery	**156**	
● Enhanced capacities and skills	**80**	
● Increased awareness and evidence-based information	**86**	
Total	**332**	

Note: ADB's support is in terms of the number of knowledge products and services planned in Viet Nam and Government's demand is the number of knowledge requests collected across ministries through demand surveys.

Source: Knowledge Advisory Services Center, Sustainable Development and Climate Change Department, Asian Development Bank.

C. Prioritize and Categorize Knowledge

1. Agree on Knowledge Outcomes Linked to Country Partnership Strategy Strategic Objective

18. The next step is for the country team to draft knowledge outcome(s) for each CPS strategic objective. Table 2 provides an example of determining knowledge outcome for each of the CPS strategic objective.

Table 2: Sample Country Partnership Strategy Strategic Objectives and Associated Knowledge Outcomes

CPS Strategic Objective	Knowledge Outcome
1. Sustainable and Inclusive Growth Enhanced	Green growth and climate resilience strengthened by providing knowledge solutions and improved capacity in planning, project preparation and implementation, financing, and monitoring.
2. Improved Human Capital	Knowledge Outcome. Improved policy design and practices for a more productive and competitive work force through strengthened public health, education, and social protection programs.
3. More Resilient, Diversified, and Productive Economy	Knowledge Outcome. Economic transformation promoted through structural reforms, better governance, and enhanced private sector led growth.

CPS = country partnership strategy,
Source: Knowledge Advisory Services Center, Sustainable Development and Climate Change Department, Asian Development Bank.

2. Prioritize Knowledge Solutions to Be Delivered Under Each Country Partnership Strategy Strategic Objective

19. The CKP team prioritizes the knowledge solutions, in consultation with the relevant departments, to ensure that these meet the knowledge outcomes of the CPS strategic objectives and the knowledge needs identified with the government. The CKP team uses the following criteria for prioritizing the knowledge solutions:

(i) What is already covered under ADB's existing portfolio of knowledge products and services (KPS) (or could be adjusted for inclusion in the existing or proposed knowledge TA portfolio)?

(ii) Are these knowledge needs aligned with the country's CPS strategic objectives?

(iii) Is this an urgent need or priority of the government?

(iv) Does the knowledge solution align with ADB's larger corporate mandates?

(v) Does ADB have the capacity to cater to the requested knowledge demand or is it a new area of work that ADB may not be able to address?

(vi) Can ADB deliver solutions largely using in-house capacity? If it is an area of work that cannot be covered by ADB, could collaboration be sought through partnerships with other multilateral development banks?

3. Agree on Focus of Knowledge Program

20. Knowledge solutions under each knowledge outcomes aligned with the CPS strategic objective should be categorized according to three knowledge result categories (Appendix 3).

    (i) **Knowledge result category 1: Increased awareness and evidence-based information.** Knowledge products that meet DMC needs through research or analytics on a particular subject, sector, or thematic area, including flagship products, technical studies, working papers, and communication support.

    (ii) **Knowledge result category 2: Improved program and/or project delivery.** KPS that support the delivery of the operational projects through customized knowledge solutions, including policy support, sector technical assistance, project feasibility studies, guidance notes and toolkits, and case study or innovation notes.

    (iii) **Knowledge result category 3: Enhanced capacities and skills.** Strengthening institutional capabilities through knowledge products that strengthen the capacity of the client government, or other stakeholders working closely with the government, to deliver development programs, including knowledge partnerships and collaborations, trainings, workshops, conferences, study trips, experts' visits, and knowledge exchanges.

21. This categorization based on knowledge results makes it easier to match the knowledge needs of the DMCs with the knowledge support from ADB. Appendix 6B provides a sample categorization of ADB's knowledge supply based on knowledge results.

22. The country team prepares a draft of the CKP supporting the CPS for its entire 5-year duration. The CKP details the knowledge

D. Draft

outcomes to be achieved (para. 17) and the associated knowledge solution categorized by knowledge results (para. 19) for each of the CPS strategic objectives. Appendix 7 provides the template for the CKP.

23. The country team meets with the government to review and validate the draft of the CKP to ensure that it has

    (i) secured buy-in of the government on the knowledge solutions being offered against each strategic objective of the CPS; and

    (ii) addressed the knowledge result categories of each knowledge solution for enhancing the impact of ADB's support.

24. The country team presents the finalized CKP to the government and prepares an aide-mémoire for signing to implement the plan in line with the CPS period.

III. Updating the Country Knowledge Plan for the Indicative Country Pipeline and Monitoring Report

25. The CKP is attached to the CPS to highlight how ADB will meet the DMCs' knowledge needs through a programmatic approach. The CKP focusses on knowledge outcomes under each of the strategic objectives of the CPS, and the associated knowledge solutions that will be delivered by ADB to meet the knowledge outcomes. While the knowledge outcomes remain constant for the duration of the CPS, the respective outputs can be revised and updated annually as part of the CKP table in the indicative country pipeline and monitoring report (ICPM). The country team confirms the updated list of knowledge solutions with the government either through a memorandum of understanding or an aide-mémoire. The annual update ensures that the CKP is dynamic to meet any emerging and just-in-time knowledge needs from the DMCs within the CPS period.

26. The CKP team can update the CKP table in the ICPM in two ways:

    (i) The team can schedule a consultation with the government on knowledge needs alongside the annual country programming mission; or

    (ii) The team can hold separate knowledge consultation with representatives of the government to identify their priority and/or upcoming knowledge needs.

The team invites representatives of the government with whom ADB works closely in implementing projects as well as other government offices that contribute to the strategic objectives of the country's CPS. The team also invites staff from ADB's sector divisions, knowledge departments, other non-operations departments, and ADBI, to be informed of the government's changing knowledge needs.

27. It is advisable to hold these consultations around the CPS strategic objectives to ensure that crosscutting knowledge needs are identified, and integrated solutions are explored.

28. During the ICPM review, the CKP team monitors which of the knowledge needs of the government are not met to inform next year's iteration of the CKP.

IV. Sustaining a Dynamic Country Knowledge Plan

29. To ensure that the CKP remains dynamic, is undertaken in a consistent manner, and is streamlined with the ICPM, ADB can consider the following administrative measures:

    (i) Appoint a focal point as the custodian of the CKP on behalf of the government.

    (ii) Appoint a focal point in ADB (within the country office or resident mission) who (a) is responsible for ensuring that the CKP is synchronized with the CPS, (b) who convenes the knowledge consultations; (c) who ensures that the client's knowledge needs are addressed by ADB, and (d) who coordinates with all ADB sector groups and departments to collate knowledge needs and solutions. The focal point also organizes the ICPM exercise for review of the CKP.

    (iii) Plan regular coordination between the CKP focal points of the government and ADB for a quick review of the CKP, analyzing the progress of ongoing knowledge solutions, identifying new knowledge needs, and reviewing solutions and their effectiveness in delivering results.

    (iv) Monitor the delivery of agreed knowledge solutions to track which of the knowledge needs are unmet, for consideration in the next year's updating of the ICPM.

The goal of the dynamic CKP is to enable ADB to formulate a strategic program that focuses on delivering quality knowledge to clients rather than mere quantity. By providing knowledge that helps DMCs solve their development challenges, this process will contribute to the thrust of Strategy 2030 in transforming ADB into a knowledge solutions provider of choice in Asia and Pacific Region.

Methodology for Analyzing Country Knowledge Portfolio

edge Plan (CKP) team can conduct detailed analysis of the portfolio generated in paras. 10-12. This analysis provides insights into the existing fo
: Bank (ADB) knowledge support. The analysis can be conducted separately for active technical assistance (TA) projects and proposed TA proje
various analysis that can be conducted on the TA project portfolio.
se whether they want to conduct the basic analysis or the advanced analysis.

Analyzing Country Knowledge Portfolio

	Basic Analysis	Advanced Analysis	Some Guiding Questi
alysis: Depicts mber and value cross years	• Overall TA projects by year (number and value) • Trend in average value of each TA project over the years	• Split of RETA and country-specific TA projects by number and value of TA projects • Split of KSTA and TRTA by number and value	• Has the size of TA projects (in $) or decreasing over the years?

idth Analysis: s of TA projects threshold	• Split of TA projects by size
	  - $0–$1 million
	  - $1 million–$2 million
	  - $2 million–$5 million
	  - more than $5 million
		• RETA and country-specific details by amount bandwidth
		• KSTA and TRTA details by amount bandwidth
			• Are there many small-value TA pr be increasing administrative and t Is there room to consolidate and/ projects?
			• Are there many small-value RETA portfolio and are these RETA proj the country?

TA Snapshot: s on the type pport, both raphic scope ntry-specific) port (KSTA vs.	• Distribution of RETA and country-specific (number and value) • Distribution of KSTA and TRTA (number and value) - Older TA projects are classified based on a different category: CDTA, PATA, PPTA, RDTA. In these cases, the TA projects should be mapped to the new category of KSTA and TRTA after reading the TA report in detail.	• Average value of RETA and country-specific TA projects • Average value of KSTA and TRTA projects • Split of KSTA and TRTA by RETA and overall country-specific TA	• Is the country being strategically projects? • Are all RETA projects relevant an country in achieving its knowledg • Would TRTA or KSTA projects be achieving the country's knowledg

CO

	Basic Analysis	Advanced Analysis	Some Guiding Qu⟨
⟨...⟩ysis: Provides ⟨...⟩the sectoral ⟨...⟩TA. The analysis ⟨...⟩data according to ⟨...⟩r mapping.	• Value and number of TA projects by sector (agriculture, natural resources, and rural development; education; energy; finance; health; industry and trade; ICT; public sector management; transport; water; and urban infrastructure) • RETA and country-specific TA projects by sector • KSTA and TRTA projects by sector	• Average value of TA projects by sector • Average value of KSTA and TRTA projects by sector • Average value of RETA and country-specific TA projects by sector • RETA vs. country-specific TA projects by sector, further split by KSTA and TRTA projects **If the portfolio is large enough,** • Split of TA projects by knowledge result category for each sector, • Split of TA projects by CPS strategic objective for each sector,	• Is the portfolio allocation acros⟨ with the country's CPS strateg⟨ • Does the portfolio allocation s⟨ structural program responding⟨ post-COVID 19 structural rec⟨
⟨...⟩ Analysis: Shows ⟨...⟩on of TA projects ⟨...⟩t	• Number and value of TA projects by department	• Average value of TA projects by department, • Split of RETA and country-specific TA projects in each department, and • Split of KSTA and TRTA projects in each department. **If the portfolio is large enough,** • Split of TA projects by knowledge result category for each department, • Split of TA projects by CPS strategic objective for each department, and • Split of TA projects by sector for each department.	• Which departments manage m⟨ country's TA portfolio? • Which departments need to c⟨ the country's knowledge outc⟨

	Basic Analysis	Advanced Analysis	Some Guiding Questio

bjective
s insights on
ts of the CPS
ost and the
	• First step is to analyze and understand the CPS document for the country. Map out the CPS strategic objectives, substrategic objectives, and crosscutting themes (if any) for the country. Thematic areas are climate change, environment, gender, governance, social development, public-private partnerships, and regional cooperation.
	
	• Link each TA to respective CPS strategic objective(s) by reading the objective and outputs of each TA. Some TA projects would align perfectly with a single CPS strategic objective, while others may align with more than one strategic objectives, or no strategic objective at all.
	
	• Categorize the TA projects based on the following CPS strategic objective categories[a]. Plot graphs to show number and value of TA projects by these categories:
	
	    - TA projects aligned with strategic objective no.;
	
	    - TA projects aligned with more than one strategic objective; and
	
	    - Overall Program TA projects: These TA projects do not align with any of the strategic objectives but are still important for the country. They are typically projects and strategic studies that help ADB better design and implement their portfolio.
	
	• Analyze if TA projects have a dominant crosscutting theme. Note that all TA projects need not have a crosscutting theme. Check allocation of TA projects (number and value) across the crosscutting themes mentioned in the country's CPS. Plot graphs to show the number and value of TA projects by CPS crosscutting theme.
	
	• Plot graphs to show the split of KSTA and TRTA projects in each CPS strategic objective.
		Plot graphs to show the following:
		
		• Split of RETA and country-specific TA projects in each CPS strategic objective;
		
		• Average value of TA projects in each CPS strategic objective;
		
		• Average value of KSTA and TRTA projects in each CPS strategic objective;
		
		• Knowledge result category, sector, and department analyses by CPS strategic objective can also be done, if required.
			• Are all CPS strategic objectives rec
			  funds?
			
			• Is there any crosscutting thematic a
			  receiving less focus?
			
			• Is there a strategy around overall p
			  projects that improve the country's
			  management and performance?

con

	Basic Analysis	Advanced Analysis	Some Guiding Qu
Results Categories provides insights on ledge outcomes are n a country	• Read the TA report in detail and map each TA to one of the following knowledge results categories (Appendix 2 provides details on knowledge result categories): - **Knowledge result category 1: Increased awareness and evidence-based information.** Knowledge products that cater to meeting DMC needs through research or analytics on a particular subject area, a sector preference, or a thematic area, including flagship products, technical studies, working papers, and communication support. - **Knowledge result category 2: Improved program/ project delivery.** Knowledge products and solutions that support the delivery of the operational projects of ADB through customized knowledge solutions, including policy support, sector technical assistance, project feasibility studies, guidance notes and toolkits, and case study or innovation notes. - **Knowledge result category 3: Enhanced capacities and skills.** Strengthening institutional capabilities through knowledge products that strengthen the capacity of the client government or other stakeholders working closely with government to deliver development programs, including knowledge partnerships and collaborations, trainings, workshops, conferences, study trips, experts' visits, and knowledge exchanges. • Plot graphs to show (i) the number and value of TA projects by knowledge results categories, and (ii) the split of KSTA and TRTA projects for each knowledge results category.	Plot graphs to show the following: • Split of RETA and country-specific TA projects in each knowledge results categories; • Average value of TA projects in each knowledge result category; • Average value of KSTA and TRTA projects in each knowledge results categories; and • CPS strategic objective, sector, and department analysis can also be done, if required.	• Is one knowledge result categ over others and is this in line v knowledge needs? • Are capacity building activitie KSTA projects or TRTA proje

pment Bank, CDTA = capacity development technical assistance, COVID-19 = coronavirus disease, CPS = country partnership strategy, DMC = developing member country, ICT = ir nology, KSTA = knowledge and support technical assistance, PATA = policy advice technical assistance, PPTA = project preparatory technical assistance, RDTA = research and devel egional technical assistance, TA = technical assistance, TRTA = transactions technical assistance.

Viet Nam were mapped to the following CPS strategic objectives for 2021: (i) strategic objective 1: green growth and climate resilience, (ii) strategic objective 2: social equity and inclu tiveness and private sector development, (iv) more than one strategic objectives, and (v) overall program TA.

Advisory Services Center, Sustainable Development and Climate Change Department, Asian Development Bank.

Mapping of Knowledge Products and Services by Knowledge Result Categories

g of Knowledge Products and Services by Knowledge Result Categories

Knowledge Support	Definition	ADB Examples	Primary Aud
What are the specific knowledge products and services that ADB provides to its clients to create better development solutions, enhance skills, and accelerate project impact and implementation?	What does the specific product/service consist of?	What are specific examples from ADB's current work?	Who (which primary clie is the specific knowledge designed for?
ERCD's Impact Evaluation	Provides guidance to readers Consists of a series of statistical techniques whose objective is to evaluate the outcomes that can be truly attributed to a project or intervention	Mumbai Metro: Transforming Transport in a Megacity	DMC officials, implemen donor community, secto experts country experts
Signature products	Knowledge products that refer to individual operational or sector/thematic priority in Strategy 2030, including knowledge management, ICT, and civil society	Fifth CAREC Railway Working Group Meeting (CWRD, 2019)	Sector/thematic experts think tanks/knowledge in development partners
Special report	Knowledge work that responds to special requests from donors, Board, DMC governments, or a felt need from internal assessment/review	Meeting Asia's Infrastructure Needs (ERCD, 2017)	DMC officials, developm donors
Case study	A detailed documentation of a project or program including its different components, implementation details, key stakeholders, lessons learned, best practices identified, and way forward	Bringing Innovation to Bus: This supported ADB Project: 40625-013: People's Republic of China: Lanzhou Sustainable Urban Transport Project Rapid Transit	DMC officials, sector/th research and academia, private sector, think tan institutes, development donors, ADB
Technical study (include books)	Presents knowledge acquired from ADB's operational and non-operational experience; request from management, DMC government	Conceptual Design of the Intelligent Transport Systems Project—Case in Gui'an New District (EARD, 2019)	DMC officials, sector/th civil society, private sect partners
ADB Working Paper Series	Felt research need, seeking new ideas and inputs in empirical studies and others relevant to ADB's operations	Upcycling Plastic Waste for Rural Road Construction in India: An Alternative Solution to Technical Challenges (SARD, 2020)	Research and academia, knowledge institutes, de partners, sector/themat
Innovation notes	Document a key innovation in a particular field, including the context of the innovation, challenges faced, key innovations, impact, key emerging lessons, and way forward	Tech for Impact website	DMC officials, sector/th research and academia, private sector, think tan institutes, development donors, ADB
Videos, infographics, multimedia features -dissemination/knowledge sharing	Use multimedia tools to capture key elements of a program or project or showcase a best practice or an innovation.	- ADB assisted Tajikistan in upgrading the road from Dushanbe to Tursunzade, connecting the country to its neighbors and opening up opportunities for trade and commerce. (CWRD, 2018) TAJ: CAREC Corridor 3 (Dushanbe–Uzbekistan Border) Improvement Project - Malolos–Clark Railway Project: North–South Commuter Railway (infographic)	DMC officials, impleme donor community, coun thematic experts, resea civil society, private sec knowledge institutes, de partners, ADB

CO

	Knowledge Support	Definition	ADB Examples	Primary A...
...e ...s?	What are the specific knowledge products and services that ADB provides to its clients to create better development solutions, enhance skills, and accelerate project impact and implementation?	What does the specific product/service consist of?	What are specific examples from ADB's current work?	Who (which primary ... is the specific knowle... designed for?
	Op-Ed	Article published in a newsletter expressing the strong opinion of an author on an issue or event	Sustainable Development and Equality: Two Sides of the Same Coin–Armida S. Alisjahbana, Bambang Susantono, and Haoliang Xu	Donor community, se... experts, research and tanks/ knowledge inst... partners
CT	Country diagnostic studies	Attempt to diagnose the most critical constraints that the country faces to achieve development plans and poverty reduction strategies	The Enabling Environment for Disaster Risk Financing in Nepal: Country Diagnostics Assessment (ERCD, 2019)	DMC officials, sector/...
	Policy brief	Short position papers to inform, stimulate debate, persuade policymakers, or generate a quick response to a policy issue	Policy Brief: A Safe Public Transportation Environment for Women and Girls (CWRD, 2015)	DMC officials, countr... thematic experts
	Assessments	Country Sector and Thematic Assessment Document the current assessment and strategic assistance priorities of ADB and the governments of its DMCs	Armenia's Transformative Urban Future: National Urban Assessment (CWRD, 2019)	DMC officials, implem... country experts, secto... development partners...
	Technical reports	Present knowledge acquired from ADB's operational and non-operational experience; request from management, DMC government	Action Plan for Promotion of Coastal Shipping in India It identifies critical infrastructure and policy interventions needed to promote coastal water-based transportation to help reduce logistics costs.	DMC officials, ADB
	Guidelines/toolkits/manuals	Detailed and step-by-step process guide that explains the implementation of a program or project including objectives of the program, methodology to be followed, key modalities and components of the project, etc.	Decision Makers' Guide to Road Tolling in CAREC Countries: This guide is part of a series of knowledge products developed to support CAREC member countries in addressing priorities in CAREC Transport and Trade Facilitation Strategy 2020.	DMC officials, implem... sector/thematic exper...
	FAQs	Document frequently asked questions about a particular program, project, or a scheme as a quick reference document		

Knowledge Support	Definition	ADB Examples	Primary Audi
What are the specific knowledge products and services that ADB provides to its clients to create better development solutions, enhance skills, and accelerate project impact and implementation?	What does the specific product/service consist of?	What are specific examples from ADB's current work?	Who (which primary clier is the specific knowledge designed for?
Lessons learned	Synthesizes key lessons drawn from evaluation and completion reports of ADB-supported projects and programs Users are advised to carefully review these lessons in the context of country, sector, and thematic area	Lessons Database	DMC officials, sector/the research and academia, c private sector, think tanks institutes, development p Donors, ADB
Data library	Central repository of all of ADB's public data (by country, by topic: sector/theme)	https://data.adb.org/	DMC officials, implemen donor community, count thematic experts, researc civil society, private secto knowledge institutes, dev partners, ADB
Social media hub ADB podcast	Highly interactive collaboration platforms	https://www.listennotes.com/podcasts/adb-pod-cast-asian-development-bank-0q4cjPUKAgo/	DMC officials, implemen donor community, count thematic experts, researc civil society, private secto knowledge institutes, dev partners, ADB
Technology innovation challenge	A contest that is aimed at finding and supporting new ideas and accelerating innovations, usually culminating in an event to recognize the winners of the competition		DMC officials, implemen country experts, sector/t research and academia, c private sector, knowledge
Technical blogs	Straight talk from development experts, written in an informal or conversational style to share expertise, views, and opinions Document projects, important programs, policies, or even a sectoral/thematic challenge; provide guidance to readers	Blogs on COVID-19	DMC officials, donor cor thematic experts, researc civil society, private secte knowledge institutes, de partners
Knowledge portals/summary explainers as part of the portal	Knowledge collaboration platforms for sharing development experience and expertise relevant to SDGs using explainers, insights, summary policy briefs, and case studies	Development Asia What the World's First Bus Rapid Transit System Can Teach Us	DMC officials, donor cor thematic experts, researc civil society, private secte knowledge institutes, de partners

co

	Knowledge Support	Definition	ADB Examples	Primary
dge nts?	What are the specific knowledge products and services that ADB provides to its clients to create better development solutions, enhance skills, and accelerate project impact and implementation?	What does the specific product/service consist of?	What are specific examples from ADB's current work?	Who (which primary is the specific knowl designed for?
	Knowledge portals/summary explainers as part of the portal	Highlight key results achieved because of a project, program, or initiative May include lessons learned and guidance for taking it forward	How to Increase the Fuel Efficiency of Road Freight Transport (EARD)	DMC officials, dono thematic experts, re civil society, private knowledge institutes partners
D	Country consultations	A facilitated series of conversations among stakeholders and peers to gain multiple perspectives and deeper understanding, reach consensus, or encourage action.		DMC officials, imple country experts, sec civil society
	Workshops/conferences/forums and proceedings	A formal event in which a large number of participants comes together to share knowledge and their experiences on a specific topic/theme	2018 Global Infrastructure Forum: Unlocking Green, Sustainable, Resilient and Inclusive Technology-Driven Infrastructure (SDCC, 2018) Viet Nam: Transport Connection in Northern Mountainous Provinces Project Training of facilitators was undertaken together with HIV/AIDS and human trafficking campaign	DMC officials, imple country experts, sec civil society, media
	Study tours/exchange visits	A visit or series of visits by a group or by an individual to one or more countries or within a country or sites, with a specific learning goal and to experience firsthand how something was or is being implemented	TA-funded study tours	DMC officials, imple country experts, sec media

Knowledge Support	Definition	ADB Examples	Primary Aud
What are the specific knowledge products and services that ADB provides to its clients to create better development solutions, enhance skills, and accelerate project impact and implementation?	What does the specific product/service consist of?	What are specific examples from ADB's current work?	Who (which primary clie is the specific knowledge designed for?
Transfer of expertise			
Secondments	**(i) Secondment In** An assignment involving qualified professionals who come to ADB on an extra-budgetary basis but who are financed by their parent organization and who retain reemployment rights with that organization **(ii) Secondment Out** Provides staff the opportunity to broaden their knowledge base in a certain sector, theme, or functional area, through a one- or two-year assignment with a partner institution		DMC officials, knowledg society
Knowledge Partnerships and Development Partnerships	**(iii) Knowledge Partnerships and Development Partnerships** Pairing of one institution with a similar peer institution, but usually with a more mature institution for learning and for a mutually beneficial partnership	ADB-Austrian Institute of Technology partnership (February 2018): The partnership supports the development of sustainable, livable, resilient, and economic competitive cities through the Cities Development Initiative for Asia (CDIA) program and contributes to ADB's capacity building for the utilization of ICT in the development of urban infrastructure solutions and services.	DMC department, imple partners, research and a society, private sector, t knowledge institutes, de partners
Sector- and thematic-specific capacity training for DMCs	Trainings imparted to client/partners for enhanced skills and knowledge for improving program/project implementation and management through face-to-face events or online/eLearning courses	Highway Development and Management System (HDM-4) Training Within ADB, HDM-4 has long been used as a basis for the economic analysis of road projects during project preparation. ADB's environment safeguard requirements	DMC officials, impleme sector/thematic experts
Data library	Central repository for all of ADB's public data (by country, by topic: sector/theme)	https://data.adb.org/	DMC officials, impleme donor community, cou thematic experts, resea civil society, private sec knowledge institutes, de partners, ADB

contin

Knowledge Support	Definition	ADB Examples	Primary
What are the specific knowledge products and services that ADB provides to its clients to create better development solutions, enhance skills, and accelerate project impact and implementation?	What does the specific product/service consist of?	What are specific examples from ADB's current work?	Who (which primary is the specific knowledge designed for?
Social media hub ADB podcast	Highly interactive collaboration platforms	https://www.listennotes.com/podcasts/adb-podcast-asian-development-bank-0q4cjPUKAgo/	DMC officials, impler donor community, co thematic experts, rese civil society, private s knowledge institutes, partners, ADB
Technology innovation challenge	A contest that is aimed at finding and supporting new ideas and accelerating innovations, usually culminating in an event to recognize the winners of the competition		DMC officials, impler country experts, secte research and academ private sector, knowle
Technical blogs	Straight talk from development experts written in an informal or conversational style to share expertise, views, and opinions Document projects, important programs, policies, or even a sectoral/thematic challenge; provides guidance to readers	Blogs on COVID-19	DMC officials, donor thematic experts, rese civil society, private se knowledge institutes, partners
Knowledge portals/summary explainers as part of the portal	Knowledge collaboration platforms for sharing development experience and expertise relevant to SDGs using explainers, insights, summary policy briefs, and case studies Highlights key results achieved because of a project, program, or initiative May include lessons learned and guidance for taking it forward	Development Asia What the World's First Bus Rapid Transit System Can Teach Us How to Increase the Fuel Efficiency of Road Freight Transport (EARD)	DMC officials, donor thematic experts, rese civil society, private se knowledge institutes, partners
Country consultations	A facilitated series of conversations among stakeholders and peers to gain multiple perspectives and deeper understanding, reach consensus, or encourage action	11th Asia-Pacific Financial Inclusion Forum: Policy Dialogue	DMC officials, implem country experts, secto civil society
Workshops/conferences/forums and proceedings	A formal event in which a large number of participants come together to share knowledge and their experiences on a specific topic/theme	2018 Global Infrastructure Forum: Unlocking Green, Sustainable, Resilient and Inclusive Technology-Driven Infrastructure (SDCC, 2018) Viet Nam: Transport Connection in Northern Mountainous Provinces Project Training of facilitators was undertaken together with HIV/AIDS and human trafficking campaign	DMC officials, implem country experts, secte civil society, media

Knowledge Support	Definition	ADB Examples	Primary Audi...
What are the specific knowledge products and services that ADB provides to its clients to create better development solutions, enhance skills, and accelerate project impact and implementation?	What does the specific product/service consist of?	What are specific examples from ADB's current work?	Who (which primary clien... is the specific knowledge designed for?
Study tours/exchange visits	A visit or series of visits by a group or individual to one or more countries or within a country or sites, with a specific learning goal and to experience firsthand how something was or is being implemented	TA-funded study tours	DMC officials, implemen... country experts, sector/t... media
Transfer of expertise Secondments	**(i) Secondment In** An assignment involving qualified professionals who come to ADB on an extra-budgetary basis but who are financed by their parent organization and who retain reemployment rights with that organization **(ii) Secondment Out** Provides staff the opportunity to broaden their knowledge base in a certain sector, theme, or functional area, through a one- or two-year assignment with a partner institution		DMC officials, knowledge... society
Knowledge Partnerships and Development Partnerships	**(iii) Knowledge Partnerships and Development Partnerships** Pairing of one institution with a similar peer institution, but usually with a more mature institution for learning and for a mutually beneficial partnership	ADB-Austrian Institute of Technology (AIT) partnership (February 2018): The partnership supports the development of sustainable, livable, resilient, and economic competitive cities through the Cities Development Initiative for Asia (CDIA) program and contributes to ADB's capacity building for the utilization of ICT in the development of urban infrastructure solutions and services.	DMC department, imple... partners, research and ac... society, private sector, th... knowledge institutes, de... partners
Sector- and thematic-specific capacity training for DMCs	Trainings imparted to client/partners for enhanced skills and knowledge for improving program/project implementation and management through face-to-face events or online/eLearning courses	Highway Development and Management System (HDM-4) Training Within ADB, HDM-4 has long been used as a basis for the economic analysis of road projects during project preparation. ADB's environment safeguard requirements	DMC officials, implemen... sector/thematic experts

ent Bank, CAREC = Central Asia Regional Economic Cooperation, COVID-19 = coronavirus disease, CWRD = Central and West Asia Department, DMC = developing member coun... tment, ERCD = Economic Research and Regional Cooperation Department, ICT = information and communication technology, SARD = South Asia Department, SDCC = Sustainab... partment, SDG = Sustainable Development Goal.

sory Services Center, Sustainable Development and Climate Change Department, Asian Development Bank.

APPENDIX 3: Sample Agenda for Sector Consultation and Turnkey E-mail

Table A3: Sample Agenda for Sector Consultation and Turnkey E-mail

PLENARY SESSION (2:00–2:25 p.m.)		
2:00–2:05 p.m.	Setting the context: Key priorities of the [Name of country] country knowledge plan (CKP)	[Name] Country Director, [Resident Mission]
2:05–2:15 p.m.	The [Name of country] CPS Overview	[Name] [Designation], [Resident Mission/ Department]
2:15–2:20 p.m.	Explaining the dynamic CKP	[Name] [Designation], [Resident Mission/ Department]
2:20–2:25 p.m.	Presentation of key findings of [Name of country] country knowledge plan analysis	[NAME] [Designation], [Resident Mission/ Department]

BREAKOUT SESSIONS (2:30 – 3:30 p.m.)		
	CPS OBJECTIVE 1: e.g., Promoting Green Growth and Climate Change	**CPS OBJECTIVE 2:** e.g., Social Equity and Inclusion	**CPS OBJECTIVE 3:** e.g., Competitiveness and Private Sector

	CPS OBJECTIVE 1	CPS OBJECTIVE 2	CPS OBJECTIVE 3
	Facilitators: [NAME], [Designation], [Resident Mission/ Department] [NAME], [Designation], [Resident Mission/ Department]	Facilitators: [NAME], [Designation], [Resident Mission/ Department] [NAME], [Designation], [Resident Mission/ Department]	Facilitators: [NAME], [Designation], [Resident Mission/ Department] [NAME], [Designation], [Resident Mission/ Department]
2:30–3:30 p.m.	Sector presentations for proposed knowledge outputs and KPS for Country Knowledge Plan 2021–2025 **2:30 - 2: 45 p.m.: Overview of the strategic objective** The breakout session will start with an overview of the overall work program, an analysis of respective TA portfolio and key areas for specialization, followed by a review of the knowledge needs as received from the government. **2:45 - 3: 20 p.m.: Sector team** Each ADB team will be given 5 minutes to provide inputs and respond to the knowledge needs (demands) from government (captured in the Knowledge Survey) and how their work program addresses/could be reoriented to meet the demands. **3: 20 - 3: 30 p.m.: Q&A**		

PLENARY SESSION (3:35–4:00 p.m.)		
3:35–3:50 p.m.	Reporting back to plenary	Facilitators
3:50–4:00 p.m.	Closing remarks and next steps	[Designation], [Resident Mission/Department]

E-mail to Invite Participants for ADB consultations

Dear Sector/Department Lead,

The Knowledge Advisory Services Center (SDCC-KC) has partnered with the [Country Resident Mission] to develop a dynamic country knowledge plan that aligns with [Government] knowledge needs as well as the portfolio of support being provided by ADB. As part of this initiative, SDCC-KC and the [Resident Mission (RM) office] have recently undertaken a review of ADB's knowledge support under the [Country CPS year–year], evaluating the alignment and relevance of its knowledge offering, with a view to improve the positioning of the knowledge support to be more dynamic, just-in-time, and responsive to client needs [if necessary, stage especially responding to urgent priorities].

Besides an overall study of the country knowledge plan of ADB, we have also carried out a sector-specific analysis of the TA offered to [name of Country]. Selected results will be shared with the [Government] and partner implementing agencies during a Knowledge Consultations Forum to be held on [date], to which you will be invited as an active participant (more details forthcoming).

However, prior to the knowledge consultations, we would like to present the findings of the sector analysis to your team, with the following objectives:

- To validate the key findings,

- To discuss the key areas of knowledge needs from the client,

- To explore how the current TA program may be reprioritized to meet the **current development challenges.**

In the coming week, we would like to schedule a meeting with you and those who lead projects being supported by TA in your sector for [country]. We have also included relevant colleagues from SDCC sector and thematic groups, ERCD, and other advisory departments as well as ADB Institute. Please feel free to include other team members who may be involved in the delivery of your sector knowledge program or correct us if we have made an error.

Would you also like us to get in touch with the following people who lead country-focused TA under [sector]: [list staff names here]

My colleague, [Name of staff], will coordinate with your team members to schedule a convenient time. Thank you and look forward to the interaction.

Regards,
[Name]

APPENDIX 4: Sample Agenda for Government Consultation and Turnkey E-mail

Please note: The sessions focus on the three strategic objectives of the Country Partnership Strategy. Participants are welcome to attend all consultations on the various substrategic objectives or choose to attend the substrategic objective most relevant to their sector, theme, or department. Invitees can also nominate relevant staff to attend the various discussions.

Table A4: Sample Agenda for Government Consultation and Turnkey E-mail

	PRESENTATION AND REVIEW OF [CPS STRATEGIC OBJECTIVE XX:] DATE XXX
5 minutes	Objectives of the consultations. Key objectives for the Country Knowledge Plan	[XXX, Country Director, RM, ADB]	
5 minutes	Opening remarks	SDCC-KC	
15 minutes	Overview of ADB Country Knowledge Plan Review of existing knowledge plan for Relevant substrategic objective Mapping Knowledge Demands from Implementing Agencies (Results of Knowledge Survey)	Speaker 2, ADB	
60 minutes Substrategic objective 1: XXXXXX Brief discussion of objective			
60 minutes	Open Forum: Government Knowledge needs 1. What are the Government priorities for knowledge products and services that ADB can collaborate/partner with? (in addition to the current KPS) 2. How could the current knowledge partnerships be strengthened?	ADB Focal: Sector Specialist Supported by: ADB staff identified	Government Agencies–Discussants List all government agencies participating under this substrategic objective
5 minutes	Summary of substrategic objective 1 and next steps	ADB Focal: Sector Specialist	
10 minutes	Break		
60 minutes Substrategic objective 2: XXXXXX Brief discussion of substrategic objective			

Sample Turnkey E-mail for Invitation to Government Consultation

DATE
Name of invitee from Government
Position
Office

Dear XXXXX,

Subject: **ADB–DMC Country Knowledge Consultation**

The Asian Development Bank (ADB) through its [name of RM] will host the [name of Country] Knowledge Consultation to discuss the [name of Country] Government's key priorities in terms of knowledge products and services. As a result of the consultation, an ADB–[name of Country] country knowledge plan (CKP) will be developed, which will identify and describe the agreed knowledge products and services with the Government of [name of Country] that ADB would collaborate and support for [Year XXXX]. The CKP would identify the implementing agency requesting the knowledge product and service, the ADB unit providing, and the source of funding, if available, and time lines for delivery.

Consultations will be divided into [Number] days corresponding to each strategic objective of the Country Partnership Strategy (CPS). Attached is the program for your reference. We would like to invite you and your colleagues to the CKP session on CPS Strategic Objective [name of strategic objective].

[Insert agenda].

In preparation for the consultations, we request your department to also present and discuss your knowledge products and requirements for [Year XXXX] . These can be in the form of knowledge studies, strategies, and capacity development, among others.

We look forward to your positive response. We would appreciate receiving your confirmation or the name of your representative on or before [date]. For any queries, please contact, [Name and position of ADB staff].

Sincerely yours,

[Name of Country Director]

APPENDIX 5: Knowledge Needs Survey Questionnaire

> **Note**
> Use this template for conducting country knowledge needs assessment survey
> red text = fill in appropriate information

KNOWLEDGE NEEDS ASSESSMENT FOR [COUNTRY NAME]

Country Knowledge Needs Assessment Survey

[Date]

Dear Colleagues,

The Asian Development Bank (ADB) is a development partner for the [Name of Country] since [Year of membership] to help advance the socioeconomic planning agenda of the country. Every year, ADB organizes its annual country programming mission, where it consults with the relevant agencies in government and agrees upon ADB's commitment and lending pipeline for that time period. ADB's knowledge solutions to Government are an integral part of our commitment to support the [Name of Country].

ADB is pleased to invite you to participate in a brief country knowledge needs assessment survey. This survey is intended to enable us to understand what knowledge solutions are required and demanded by the different agency counterparts of government, especially to address challenges brought about by [for example, the current coronavirus disease (COVID-19) pandemic.]

The findings of the survey will define the scope of knowledge-related activities to be incorporated into the Country Knowledge Plan (CKP). Knowing what the counterpart agencies need in terms of knowledge solutions and products will help the government of [Name of Country] and ADB to design and implement better programs and interventions that are innovative and integrated to answer current demands.

We would appreciate it if you could complete this survey by [Date]. The feedback you provide will be very useful for us during the knowledge consultations to be held on [Date].

We thank you for your time in completing this survey.

If you have any questions or queries related to this survey, please contact: [E-mail address].

Kind regards,
[Country Director]
[Resident Mission]
Asian Development Bank

Knowledge Needs Assessment: Survey [Year]

Name of Department and Division: _____

Contact Information: _____

1. **What is the most important knowledge support (result) that your department/agency would like to achieve in [State relevant time period]?**
   (Select top two most relevant)

   (i) <u>Improved program and/or project delivery</u> including initiatives and efforts to facilitate or improve the delivery and implementation of projects and programs (for example, new and enhanced actions, designs, processes, strategies and systems, and monitoring frameworks as well as improving efficiency through the introduction of innovations and strengthened collaborations).

   (ii) <u>Increased awareness and evidence-based information</u> through initiatives and efforts that support raised awareness, changed mindsets and attitudes, or an increased understanding of program/project interventions to improve their implementation (for example, good practice documents, knowledge and experience exchanges, research, and analysis on innovative solutions, etc.).

   (iii) <u>Enhanced capacities and skills</u> that support government departments and organizations to acquire, strengthen and maintain institutional capacities and capabilities to address a specific project-related problem or challenge.

2. **What knowledge solution would you propose to meet your department's/agency's knowledge outcome indicated in Question 1? (Please list the specific knowledge products or services.)**

Type of Knowledge Support Requested	Proposed Specific Knowledge Solution that ADB Could Potentially Support
Improved program/project delivery	
Increased awareness and evidence-based information	
Enhanced skills and capacities	
Others	

3. **Are there any specific knowledge collaborations or partnerships that could help address the above-mentioned support and the pre-identified knowledge outcomes?**
   _____
   _____
   _____
   _____
   _____
   _____

4. **Please list any ongoing or similar activities already underway in your department/agency to meet the proposed knowledge solution in Question 2?**
   i. _____
   ii. _____
   iii. _____
   iv. _____

5. **Please provide an indicative list of areas of knowledge support provided by other partners to your agency/department indicated in question 2?**
   i. World Bank _____
   ii. UN agencies_____
   iii. DFAT _____
   iv. USAID _____
   v. WHO _____
   vi. Others _____

APPENDIX 6: Matching Knowledge Needs from Government with Knowledge Solutions from ADB

A. Categorizing Knowledge Demand and ADB's Knowledge Support by Country Partnership Strategy Strategic Objective

The team categorizes knowledge needs from government and the consolidated list of Knowledge Solutions that the respective Asian Development Bank (ADB) teams have planned according to the strategic objectives of the country partnership strategy (CPS). An indicative example for one CPS strategic objective, "Improved Human Capital," is illustrated in Table A6.1.

Table A6: Example of Matching Knowledge Needs and Solutions with Country Partnership Strategy Strategic Objective

CPS Strategic Objective	Knowledge Outcome	Knowledge solutions from ADB for Upcoming Year	Knowledge needs from Government
Improved Human Capital	Improved policy design and practices for a more productive and competitive work force through strengthened public health, education and social protection programs	1. Knowledge exchange on social protection programs (2022) 2. Training program for capacitating health and nutrition professionals of primary health care units 3. Strategies and inputs on COVID-19 introducing vaccination program and roll out 4. Skills sector development plan formulated for TVET sector 5. Capacity building for developing social inclusiveness and responsiveness policies in education, health, and TVET sectors 6. Policy dialogue on improving social protection schemes especially targeting the elderly	1. Improving policies for inclusive social protection schemes 2. Assessment of COVID-19 impact 3. Capacity building for developing social inclusiveness and COVID-19 responsiveness policies in education, health and TVET sectors

ADB = Asian Development Bank, COVID-19 = coronavirus disease, CPS = country partnership strategy, TVET = technical and vocational education and training.

APPENDIX 7: Updated Country Knowledge Plan Table

{Read and delete:

(i) For guidance in preparing this appendix, refer to the Country Knowledge Plan (CKP) manual.

(ii) Teams can add a list of the new and ongoing knowledge solutions or knowledge products and services (KPS) planned and cluster these to convey how to achieve each knowledge outcome. In each indicative country pipeline and monitoring (ICPM) report, the team annually updates the summary of knowledge outputs by clustering list of proposed KPS associated with each knowledge outcome as appropriate to (a) respond to any changes in country priorities or context; (b) adjust knowledge outcomes, only if it is absolutely necessary, to improve their effectiveness based on lessons learned during the country partnership strategy (CPS) period; and (c) respond to new client needs and requests for just-in-time support.

(iii) Classify the clustered KPS according to the three knowledge results categories and outputs: (a) "improved program or project delivery" includes policy support, sector technical assistance, project-level feasibility studies, guidance notes, toolkits, and case study or innovation notes; (b) "enhanced capacities and skills, includes knowledge partnerships, trainings, workshops and conferences, and study tours and exchange visits; and (c) "increased awareness and evidence-based information" includes flagship products, technical studies, special reports, working papers, evaluations, and communication support. In case a particular knowledge solution is crosscutting two or more result areas, please prioritize according to primary knowledge result categories. (*link to understand where each knowledge solution gets classified according to knowledge result areas)

(iv) Consider only ongoing or upcoming KPS when completing in the knowledge table. Do not include knowledge solutions that have already been completed.

(v) If a knowledge solution is funded through technical assistance (TA) project(s), specify the corresponding TA number(s). If desired, the TA title can also be specified. If several knowledge solutions listed sequentially are funded by the same TA, the TA number may be listed at the top of the KPS list.

(vi) Knowledge solution not funded by TA can also be included in the CKP table.

(vii) A TA project can contribute to more than one CPS objectives and may also deliver knowledge solution under more than one knowledge results categories or outputs.

ADB = Asian Development Bank, COVID-19 = coronavirus disease, CPS = country partnership strategy, TVET = technical and vocational education and training.

Table A7: Updated Country Knowledge Plan Table for {next year}

CPS Objective 1: {Specify the objective}
Knowledge Outcome: {Describe in one or two sentences the intended knowledge outcome for this CPS objective. A knowledge outcome is the benefit from using or applying the knowledge outputs.}

Knowledge Results Categories and Outputs		
Improved Program/Project Delivery	**Enhanced capacities and skills**	**Increased Awareness and Evidence-Based Information**
Briefly describe the specific results that a cluster of KPS intend to achieve in support of the knowledge outcome. Below this, list the supporting knowledge solutions … Clustered KPS: • Supporting knowledge outputs (TA number, if applicable) • Supporting knowledge outputs (TA number, if applicable)	*Briefly describe the specific results that a cluster of KPS intend to achieve in support of the knowledge outcome. Below this, list the supporting knowledge solutions …* Clustered KPS: • Supporting knowledge outputs (TA number, if applicable) • Supporting knowledge outputs (TA number, if applicable)	*Briefly describe the specific results that a cluster of KPS intend to achieve in support of the knowledge outcome. Below this, list the supporting knowledge solutions …* Clustered KPS: • Supporting knowledge outputs (TA number, if applicable) • Supporting knowledge outputs (TA number, if applicable)

CPS objective 2: {Specify the objective}
Knowledge Outcome: {Describe in one or two sentences the intended knowledge outcome for this CPS objective.}

Knowledge Results Categories and Outputs		
Improved Program/Project delivery	**Enhanced Capacities and Skills**	**Increased awareness and evidence-based information**
Briefly describe the specific results that a cluster of KPS intend to achieve in support of the knowledge outcome. Below this, list the supporting knowledge solutions … Clustered KPS: • Supporting knowledge outputs (TA number, if applicable) • Supporting knowledge outputs (TA number, if applicable)	*Briefly describe the specific results that a cluster of KPS intend to achieve in support of the knowledge outcome. Below this, list the supporting knowledge solutions …* Clustered KPS: • Supporting knowledge outputs (TA number, if applicable) • Supporting knowledge outputs (TA number, if applicable)	*Briefly describe the specific results that a cluster of KPS intend to achieve in support of the knowledge outcome. Below this, list the supporting knowledge solutions …* Clustered KPS: • Supporting knowledge outputs (TA number, if applicable) • Supporting knowledge outputs (TA number, if applicable)

CPS objective 3: {Specify the objective}
Knowledge Outcome: {Describe in one or two sentences the intended knowledge outcome for this CPS objective.}

Knowledge Results Categories and Outputs		
Improved Program/Project delivery	**Enhanced Capacities and Skills**	**Increased awareness and evidence-based information**
Briefly describe the specific results that a cluster of KPS intend to achieve in support of the knowledge outcome. Below this, list the supporting knowledge solutions … Clustered KPS: • Supporting knowledge outputs (TA number, if applicable) • Supporting knowledge outputs (TA number, if applicable)	*Briefly describe the specific results that a cluster of KPS intend to achieve in support of the knowledge outcome. Below this, list the supporting knowledge solutions …* Clustered KPS: • Supporting knowledge outputs (TA number, if applicable) • Supporting knowledge outputs (TA number, if applicable)	*Briefly describe the specific results that a cluster of KPS intend to achieve in support of the knowledge outcome. Below this, list the supporting knowledge solutions …* Clustered KPS: • Supporting knowledge outputs (TA number, if applicable) • Supporting knowledge outputs (TA number, if applicable)

{Either define abbreviations within the table or list them alphabetically and define them below the table. Use a consistent approach and do not define some in the table and others below the table.} CPS = country partnership strategy, TA = technical assistance.

Source{s}: {List table source(s)}.